The Sea

Anton Chekhov, Russian dramatist and short-story writer, was born in 1860, the son of a grocer and the grandson of a serf. After graduating in medicine from Moscow University in 1884, he began to make his name in the theatre with the one-act comedies *The Bear, The Proposal* and *The Wedding*. His earliest full-length plays, *Ivanov* (1887) and *The Wood Demon* (1889), were not successful, and *The Seagull*, produced in 1896, was a failure until a triumphant revival by the Moscow Art Theatre in 1898. This was followed by *Uncle Vanya* (1899), *Three Sisters* (1901) and *The Cherry Orchard* (1904), shortly after the production of which Chekhov died. The first English translations of his plays were performed within five years of his death.

Martin Crimp was born in 1956. His plays include *Definitely the Bahamas* (1987), *Dealing with Clair* (1988), *Play with Repeats* (1989), *No One Sees the Video* (1990), *Getting Attention* (1991), *The Treatment* (winner of the 1993 John Whiting Award), *Attempts on Her Life* (1997), *The Country* (2000), *Face to the Wall* (2002), *Cruel and Tender* (2004) and *Fewer Emergencies* (2005). He has also translated works by Ionesco, Koltès, Genet, Marivaux and Molière.

also by Martin Crimp

MARTIN CRIMP PLAYS ONE
(*Dealing with Clair, Play with Repeats,
Getting Attention, The Treatment*)

MARTIN CRIMP PLAYS TWO
(*No One Sees the Video, The Misanthrope,
Attempts on Her Life, The Country*)

THREE ATTEMPTED ACTS
(in *Best Radio Plays of 1985*)

CRUEL AND TENDER

FEWER EMERGENCIES
(*Whole Blue Sky, Face to the Wall,
Fewer Emergencies*)

Translations

THE CHAIRS (Ionesco)
ROBERTO ZUCCO (Koltès)
THE MAIDS (Genet)
THE TRIUMPH OF LOVE (Marivaux)
THE FALSE SERVANT (Marivaux)

ANTON CHEKHOV

The Seagull

in a version by
MARTIN CRIMP

*based on a literal translation
and critical commentary by
Helen Rappaport*

faber and faber

First published in 2006
by Faber and Faber Limited
3 Queen Square, London WC1N 3AU

Typeset by Country Setting, Kingsdown, Kent CT14 8ES
Printed in England by Bookmarque Ltd, Croydon, Surrey

A CIP record for this book
is available from the British Library

ISBN 978-0-571-23466-0
ISBN 0-571-23466-6

2 4 6 8 10 9 7 5 3 1

The Seagull was first presented in this version in the Lyttelton auditorium of the National Theatre, London, on 17 June 2006. The cast was as follows:

Irina Arkádina Juliet Stevenson
Konstantin Trepliev Ben Whishaw
Piotr Sorin Gawn Grainger
Nina Zaréchnaya Hattie Morahan
Ilya Shamraev Michael Gould
Polina Shamraev Liz Kettle
Masha Shamraev Sandy McDade
Aleksei Trigorin Mark Bazeley
Evgenyi Dorn Angus Wright
Semyon Medviedenko Justin Salinger
Yakov Sean Jackson
Servants James Bolt, Beth Fitzgerald, Jonah Russell

Director Katie Mitchell
Set Designer Vicki Mortimer
Costume Designer Nicky Gillibrand
Lighting Designer Chris Davey
Movement Director Struan Leslie
Music Simon Allen
Sound Designer Christopher Shutt

Characters

Irina Arkádina
an actress

Konstantin Trepliev
her son

Piotr Sorin
her brother

Nina Zaréchnaya
a young woman, daughter of a rich landowner

Ilya Shamraev
a retired lieutenant, manages Sorin's farm

Polina Shamraev
his wife

Masha Shamraev
her daughter

Aleksei Trigorin
a writer of successful fiction

Evgenyi Dorn
a doctor

Semyon Medviedenko
a teacher

Yakov
a workman

Cook

Maid

THE SEAGULL

The action takes place on Sorin's country estate.
Two years pass between Acts Three and Four.

Act One

*Evening. A terrace at the back of the house on Sorin's
estate. Upstage is the rest of the house. Downstage—
i.e., in the space occupied by the auditorium—must be
imagined a lake. On the terrace, Yakov and other servants
are making arrangements to stage Konstantin's play. This
involves curtaining off part of the terrace, and bringing
out a grand piano. The audience for Konstantin's play
will face the lake—and therefore face the auditorium.*

Medviedenko (*off*) And the way you dress—

Masha (*off*) What d'you mean: the way I dress?

Enter Masha and Medviedenko.

Medviedenko In black—why d'you always go round in
black?

Masha I'm in mourning for my life. I'm unhappy.

Medviedenko Oh? (*Slight pause.*) Then I'm confused.
You're healthy—your father's got money—not much
money but money all the same—while after deductions
I take home less than two hundred and fifty a month.
I lead a much harder life than you do, but I don't go
round in black.

Masha It's nothing to do with money. You can be poor
and still happy.

Medviedenko Well maybe in theory—but in practice it
goes like this: there's me, my mother, my two sisters and
my baby brother living on less than two hundred and
fifty a month. So what are you suggesting? Give up

3

smoking? Stop drinking tea? Or perhaps we could just /
not eat.

Masha The play should be starting soon.

Medviedenko Oh yes. Konstantin's play. Which Nina is
going to act in. They're obsessed with each other and
doing a play together is going to cement their relationship.
Whereas the two of us don't even *have* a relationship.
I love you, Masha, which is why I can't just sit at home
vegetating. I walk here every day—two hours here, two
hours back—and what's my reward?—total indifference.
But of course, nobody wants to marry a man who can't
provide.

Masha Rubbish. (*Lights cigarette.*) I'm touched by your
love but I can't reciprocate, that's all. (*Offers cigarette.*)
Want one?

Medviedenko Not in the mood.

Pause.

Masha It's close—feels like there'll be a storm tonight.
It's just you're always picking away at things or
talking about money. I know you think poverty's the
biggest disaster in the world, but there are worse things
in life than wandering the streets begging—believe me.
I'm sorry. I know that's hard for you to understand.

Enter Sorin and Konstantin.

Konstantin I'm afraid we're not quite ready for you yet.
I'm going to have to ask you both to leave. We'll call
you when / it's time.

Sorin Masha—sweetheart—would you please please ask
that father of yours to untie the dog so it doesn't howl.
My sister spent the whole night awake again.

Masha Talk to my father yourself—it's not my job. And

4

I'm not your sweetheart. (*to Medviedenko*) Come on—
let's go.

Medviedenko (*to Konstantin*) You will tell us when it's
going to start, yes?

Sorin Of course we will.

They go out.

So now that dog will be howling all night again.

Yakov Excuse me, sir—we're going to get changed.

Konstantin Alright—but I want you in position . . .
(*Looks at watch.*) . . . ten minutes from now.

Yakov You're the boss.

Yakov and workmen go out.

Konstantin So—what d'you think—empty space—no
scenery—just the lake and the horizon. Pure theatre. The
moon's due up at exactly half past eight—which is when
we start.

Sorin Excellent.

Konstantin And if Nina's late—which she looks like
being—then the whole effect's ruined. (*rearranging Sorin*)
Christ you're a mess. Can't you do something about this
hair?

Sorin It's the tragedy of my life. Even when I was young
I looked like an alcoholic. Complete failure with women.
  What's wrong with your mother?

Konstantin Wrong? She's bored. And she's jealous. She's
got it in for me and she's got it in for my play because
I've given the part to Nina and not to her. She hasn't read
my play of course but she already hates it.

Sorin (*laughs*) Come on: you're / overreacting.

Konstantin She can't bear the thought of Nina not her getting all the attention—even in something so small scale. Because it's not as if my mother isn't a sensitive and intelligent person who genuinely cares about the world—but try saying something nice to her about another actress . . . big mistake. Nice things can be said *only about her.* Magazine features written *only about her.* She needs to have people constantly raving about her heartbreaking Cordelia or her 'waif-like' Juliet—and because out here in the country she's no way of feeding her addiction she gets bored and angry—we're all her enemies—we're all to blame. And talk about mean. We both know for a fact she's got a good seven hundred thousand stashed away in a Black Sea bank account—but ask her for money and she has a fit.

Sorin Come on—your mother worships you.

Konstantin (*laughs*) Worships me? I don't think so. She still sees herself as some kind of party-going *femme fatale*—but the problem is she's got a twenty-five-year-old son. When I'm not around she's only thirty-two—but when I'm here she's forty-three—and she hates me for it. Plus she knows I detest her darling theatre. She loves it—imagines it's her sacred contribution to society—but if you ask me this theatre of hers is death. When the curtain goes up on yet another adapted novel or some piece of vapid social commentary masquerading as art—when shouting and banging the scenery is mistaken for good acting—when writers think that dialogue means the fluent exchange of platitudes—when I see people churn out the same theatrical clichés time after time after time after time after time, then I want to scream and scream—like the man in Munch's picture.

Sorin We still need theatre.

Konstantin But we need to start again—if we can't start again from scratch—start again, make new forms—

better to completely stop. (*Looks at watch.*) I love my mother—love her to death—but her life's meaningless—trailing round after her novelist friend—name all over the papers—I'm sick of it. Yes, I realise some of it's egotistical: when I find myself thinking how much happier I'd be if she wasn't famous, if she was just a run-of-the-mill mother blah blah blah. And of course I used to feel so stupid when all her celebrity artist people turned up at her flat and I'd be the only nonentity—tolerated simply because I was her son. Because what could I say about myself? No special skills. No money. And because I'd been stupid enough to play politics at university, not even a degree. So when all these artists and writers deigned to show an interest I always knew that what they were actually doing was putting me in my place.

Sorin So what d'you make of this novelist friend? He doesn't say much.

Konstantin He's a nice enough person—hugely successful—but hardly a major talent. Put it this way—if you've read Tolstoy, you don't need to read Trigorin.

Sorin I'd be happy to settle for a minor talent—or any talent at all come to / think of it.

Konstantin Listen! (*Hugs his uncle.*) She's incredible. Even her footsteps sound beautiful—don't you think?

 Nina enters.

Nina . . . You look amazing.

Nina Am I late? Promise me I'm not late—

Konstantin No no no no no . . .

Nina I've been worrying all day—I was so scared. I thought my father would stop me coming—then he and my stepmother went out. The sky's red—the moon's already rising—and there's me driving the horse on and on and on . . . (*Laughs.*) I'm so happy. (*Squeezes Sorin's hand.*)

Sorin Those pretty eyes look more like they've been crying.

Nina It's nothing—just out of breath—in half an hour I need to get back—so please let's hurry—please—please don't make me late—my father doesn't know I'm here.

Konstantin Then let's call everyone and start.

Sorin Let me. (*He moves off, humming.*)

Nina I shouldn't be here. They think I'll be corrupted. But I'm drawn here to the lake—like a seagull. (*Looks around.*)

Konstantin We're alone.

Nina Somebody's there.

Konstantin No one.

They kiss.

Nina What's that tree?

Konstantin An elm.

Nina Why's it so dark?

Konstantin It's evening—everything's dark. Please stay for longer.

Nina No.

Konstantin Or I could come to your house.

Nina No.

Konstantin I love you.

Nina Shh . . .

Enter Yakov.

Konstantin Yakov.

Yakov Yes sir?

Konstantin Final checks, please. We're about to start.

Yakov Yes sir.

Konstantin And remember: the sulphur and the splashing noise have the same cue. (*to Nina*) Nervous?

Nina Very. It's not so much your mother—but acting in front of Aleksei Trigorin—the writer—I'm terrified. He's so famous. Is he young?

Konstantin Yes.

Nina His stories are wonderful.

Konstantin (*cold*) Are they? I've never read them.

Nina Your play's so difficult to act. My character's not real.

Konstantin Not real? I've told you: the material world is an illusion—what counts is the world of dreams.

Nina And nothing really happens—it's all talking.

They move off.

And I'm not sure a play's really a play unless it has some kind of message . . . Don't you think? . . .

They go out.

Konstantin (*off*) A message?

Nina (*off*) Yes. About love or . . . I don't know . . . people's feelings . . . relationships.

Konstantin laughs.

Why's that funny? . . .

Enter Polina and Dorn.

Polina It's getting damp. Go back and get your overcoat.

Dorn I'm hot.

Polina Why won't you look after yourself? You're so stubborn. You know damp air's bad for you, but you just like making me worry. Yesterday you spent the whole evening out on this terrace quite deliberately . . .

Dorn hums a little tune.

. . . but I suppose you found your little conversation with Irina Arkádina so totally fascinating you didn't notice the cold. Am I right?

Dorn I'm fifty-five.

Polina So? That's not old for a man. You certainly don't look old and women still find you attractive—as you very well know.

Dorn So what are you suggesting I do?

Polina Why're men all so obsessed by actresses? Mmm?

Dorn (*hums a little tune, then*) If people idealise performers and tend to treat them differently from—say—pig-farmers, then that's just how the world operates. It's outside of our control.

Polina Women have always been all over you—I suppose you can't control that either.

Dorn (*shrugs*) What if they have? Women've always been very good to me—of course—but mainly because they could trust me professionally. Ten, fifteen years ago, as you very well know, I was the only reliable obstetrician this district had. It doesn't mean I've abandoned you. Or Masha either.

Polina (*grasps his hand*) I'm sorry. I know you haven't.

Dorn Don't. Someone's coming. (*He frees his hand.*)

Konstantin enters.

Konstantin Yakov. Hurry up. The moon.

Yakov closes the curtain, shutting off a portion of the terrace and concealing Polina and Dorn. As Nina prepares to perform the play, enter unseen behind the curtain Arkádina, Sorin, Trigorin, Shamraev, Medviedenko and Masha.

Shamraev You should've seen her when was it—fifteen—no I tell a lie—twenty—it was twenty years ago I first saw you at the Poltava Agricultural Show. Amazing acting. Even in a place like that. And that colleague of yours—the comic actor—Pavel something—brilliant in Ostrovsky—Pavel Chadin—whatever happened to him?

Arkádina You keep asking me about dinosaurs. How should I know?

Shamraev Chadin . . . Pavel Chadin. There's no one like that left. The theatre's gone downhill. In the past there were mighty oaks—now all we see are the stumps.

Dorn There may be fewer geniuses about, but the average actor has significantly improved.

Shamraev I don't agree. Still—it's a matter of taste. For which—as the poet says—there is no accounting.

Konstantin pokes his head through the curtain.

Arkádina Aren't you starting?

Konstantin One more minute. Give me a chance.

Arkádina
'What have I done, that thou dar'st wag thy tongue
In noise so rude against me?'

11

Konstantin
                              'Such an act
That blurs the grace and blush of modesty.'

Yakov makes a sound cue.

*Konstantin goes through the curtain, leaving only
Nina and the servants who are stage-managing the
play visible to the audience.*

Ready everyone? Then let's begin.

Spirits
night-time spirits of the lake
rock us asleep and let us dream
of things a hundred million years from now.

Sorin A hundred million years from now there won't be
anything.

Konstantin Then let's see what not anything looks like.

Arkádina Yes let's. We're asleep.

*The curtain opens, revealing Arkádina, Trigorin,
Sorin, Polina, Shamraev, Masha, Medviedenko and
Dorn. Konstantin goes to the piano and accompanies
Nina as she speaks.*

Nina
Everything human, everything animal, every plant,
stem, green tendril, blade of grass—
each living cell
has divided and divided and divided
and died.
For millions of years
now this earth is ash, this lake thick like mercury.
No boat lands on the empty shore.
No wading bird stands in the shallows.
And the moon—look—picks her way

like a looter through the ruined houses of the dead
slicing open her white fingers
on the sheets of smashed glass—
COLD
BLANK
DISTANT.

Pause.

The brutal material struggle of individuals has ended.
Only the steady heartbeat of the world goes on.
I am that heartbeat.
I am the blood moving under the skin.
I am the slow pulse of the universal will.

Yakov does a lighting effect.

Arkádina (*sotto voce*) Is this one of those experimental
things?

Konstantin Mother!

Nina
I am alone.
Once in a hundred thousand years I try to speak
but my mouth fills with brick-dust and broken glass.
Nobody hears me:
not the moon
not the pale fires ringing the cracked horizon—
billions of atoms chaotically changing.
Only the steady heartbeat of the world does not
change.
SLOW
DEEP
IMPLACABLE.

*Pause. Sound of the Other approaching through the
water. A cloud of gas is released.*

Nina turns to face the lake.

And now my enemy approaches:
the violent Other—
origin of material brutality.

I can hear his body
    churn the lake—
smell his foul breath.
I can see his terrifying
    lidless eyes.
The violent Other:
hoping to wind the
    steel wire of reason
round my white throat.

HARD
BITTER
RESTLESS.

Arkádina I can smell sulphur. Is that intentional?

Konstantin Yes.

Arkádina (*laughs*) Of course—it's a special effect!

Konstantin Mother!

Polina (*to Dorn*) Why did you take your hat off? Put it back on or you'll catch cold.

Arkádina The doctor is doffing his hat to the violent Other, origin of / material brutality.

Konstantin Stop! Stop the play!

Arkádina What're you so / angry about?

Konstantin Stop the play! Stop it now! Stop!

The play stops.

Yakov bundles Nina off.

Forgive me. I forgot that writing and acting is the privilege of the chosen few—whose monopoly I've somehow infringed. But I . . . I . . . (*He struggles to speak, makes a gesture—'Why bother?'—and goes out.*)

Arkádina What on earth is he talking about?

Sorin Sweetheart—you hurt his pride.

Arkádina How?

Sorin You humiliated him.

Arkádina Humiliated him? He's the one who came and told me it was just for fun so that's exactly how I treated it.

Sorin Yes, but / the thing is—

Arkádina *Then* it turns out it's meant to be a great work of art. Doing his little show and choking us all with poison gas isn't in fact remotely 'just for fun'—it's a lesson in how to write and what to act in—or in other words completely boring. I understand what you're saying, but I'm not prepared to be constantly got at. He's ungracious and conceited.

Sorin He wanted to please you.

Arkádina Really? Then why didn't he choose a normal play? Why force us to sit through his experimental mumbo-jumbo? If it really was 'just for fun'—fine— I could put up with it. But he obviously thinks he's 'reinventing the form'—'revolutionising' the theatre— when he's not revolutionising anything, just being thoroughly obnoxious.

Trigorin A writer can only write what a writer writes.

Arkádina He's welcome to write what a writer writes— just leave me out of it.

Dorn But you don't have to be so angry.

Arkádina I'll be what I like, thank you very much. (*Lights cigarette.*) And I'm not angry, just upset to see my son wasting his life. I wasn't trying to humiliate him.

Medviedenko You can't really separate the spiritual from the material because the spiritual may turn out to *be* material at the atomic level. (*to Trigorin*) But what someone should really write a play about is what it's like being a schoolteacher. It's hard—life's hard.

Arkádina You're right—but no more talking about plays or atomic levels. What a beautiful evening. Is someone playing music?

They listen.

How lovely.

Polina It's on the other side.

Pause.

Arkádina (*to Trigorin*) Ten, fifteen years ago—here—on this lake—there was always music and singing—almost every evening. On that shore opposite, there were six big houses—people laughing—noise—guns going off—and love affairs, endless love affairs . . . And the young man most in demand—in fact idolised at all six—was none other than . . . (*Indicates Dorn.*) my good friend the doctor here. Today still highly attractive—but in those days irresistible.

Why did I upset poor Konstantin like that?
(*Calls.*) Konstantin! Kostya! Konstantin!

Masha I'll go and look for him.

Arkádina Would you?

Masha (*going off, calling*) Hello? Konstantin? Hello?

Nina comes out.

Nina We're obviously not going on—I might as well come out. (*Kisses Arkádina and Polina.*)

Sorin Bravo! Bravo!

Arkádina Bravo! Bravo! We thought you were wonderful: the way you look—that gorgeous voice—it's criminal to be stuck out here in the country. You have real talent. I'm serious. You owe it to yourself to act.

Nina That's my dream. But it will never happen.

Arkádina Who can say?

There's someone I'd like you to meet: Aleksei Trigorin.

Nina I'm so thrilled . . . I read everything you write.

Arkádina Don't be embarrassed. He's famous but he's still just a normal human being. You see—he's as embarrassed as you are.

A gust of wind blows the curtain.

Dorn Can we get this curtain hooked up? It's giving me the creeps.

Shamraev (*calls*) Yakov—can we hook up this curtain?

Yakov comes and hooks up the curtain.

Nina (*to Trigorin*) Weird play—don't you think?

Trigorin Didn't understand a word. But enjoyed watching it. You acted so truthfully. And the scenery was wonderful.

Pause.

Must be a lot of fish in this lake.

Nina Yes.

Trigorin I love fishing. Nothing gives me greater pleasure than sitting on a river bank at the end of a day just watching the float.

Nina But doesn't your own creative pleasure make all other pleasures irrelevant?

Arkádina (*laughing*) Be careful. When people use words like creative he has a tendency to cringe.

Shamraev I remember being at the Moscow Opera when Silva was going for bottom C. One of the basses from our own church choir happened to be up in the gallery and we were suddenly amazed to hear coming from the gallery 'Bravo Silva!'—a whole octave lower. Like this (*deep bass voice*) Bravo Silva! . . . (*normal voice*) The whole audience froze.

Pause.

Dorn Someone just passed over our graves.

Nina I have to go.

Arkádina Where? It's too early. We won't let you.

Nina My father will be waiting.

Arkádina That man . . . hmm . . .

They kiss.

But what can we do? It's a shame—a real shame to let you go.

Nina If only you knew how hard it is for me to leave.

Arkádina Someone should see you home, you poor thing.

Nina (*alarmed*) No no.

Sorin Please stay.

Nina I can't.

Sorin Stay one more hour. Come on. Say yes.

Nina (*thinks—and forces herself not to cry*) Impossible. (*Squeezes his hand and quickly goes out.*)

Arkádina That girl's been so unlucky. Turns out her mother left a vast fortune to her father and now her father's already willed it all to his second wife—leaving her quite literally with nothing. Outrageous.

Dorn Yes, I think we can safely say her darling father's a complete bastard.

Sorin (*rubbing hands*) Come on friends—let's all go. It's beginning to drizzle. My legs hurt.

Arkádina 'The wonder is he hath endur'd so long.'
Come on, you old wreck. (*Takes his arm.*)

Shamraev (*offers arm to his wife*) Madame?

Sorin That dog's howling again. (*to Shamraev*) My dear
Ilya, would you please please get someone to untie that
dog.

Shamraev Not possible—sorry—thieves might break
into the barn. I've got millet in there. (*Walks beside
Medviedenko.*) A whole octave lower—'Bravo Silva!'
Just an ordinary member of a church choir.

Medviedenko And how much d'you reckon an ordinary
member of a church choir gets paid? . . .

They all go out, except for Dorn.

Shamraev (*off*) I'm not sure they *do* get paid.

Medviedenko (*off*) Well there must be something—an
allowance—free meals . . .

Konstantin appears.

Konstantin They've all gone, then.

Dorn I'm here.

Konstantin Masha's been all over the grounds looking
for me. I can't stand her.

Dorn Konstantin—I really enjoyed your play. A bit
weird—and I don't know how it ends—but it made a
real impression. When she was talking like that about
being alone . . . the ruined houses . . . then the thing
about steel wire . . . my hands were shaking. You're a
talented person and you mustn't give up.

Konstantin takes his hand and hugs him.

Come on—stop looking so tense—please don't cry. What
is it I'm trying to say? . . . What was so good was that

you . . . weren't afraid to tackle a really big idea. Which I admire.

What's wrong?

Konstantin So you think I should carry on?

Dorn Of course. But make sure you focus on the things that really matter. Because look at me—I've had plenty of enjoyment out of life—don't get me wrong—I'm not complaining. But if I'd ever had the chance like you to be truly creative then I'd've lived in a completely different way. D'you know what I mean? Not so material.

Konstantin Uh-hu. Where's Nina?

Dorn The other thing is is be clear you've got something to say. Because however talented you are, if you don't have anything to say, you'll end up just drifting, and hating yourself.

Konstantin (*more emphatic*) Where's Nina?

Dorn She went home.

Konstantin (*in despair*) What d'you mean, went home? I have to see her. I can't not see her.

Dorn Hey hey hey—calm / down.

Konstantin I can't not see her. I can't.

    Enter Masha.

Masha Konstantin, please come indoors. Your mother's waiting. She's worried.

Konstantin Tell her I'm not here. And please will you stop following me around. You make me sick.

Dorn Hey hey hey—don't talk to her like that.

Konstantin (*through tears*) Goodbye Doctor. Thank you. (*He goes.*)

Dorn He doesn't mean it.

Masha That's what people always say when somebody's telling the truth. (*Takes out cigarettes.*)

Dorn (*takes her cigarettes and throws them into the bushes*) That's disgusting.

　Pause.

D'you think they're dancing? Let's go inside.

Masha Please wait.

Dorn What?

Masha Can I just talk to you for a moment? Please? (*becoming agitated*) My father doesn't care. You're the only person I can say this to. Help me. Please help me or I'm going to do something really stupid—mess up my life . . .

Dorn What d'you mean? Help you how?

Masha It hurts so much. Nobody knows how much it hurts.
　I'm in love with Konstantin.

Dorn What's making you all so tense? And so love-obsessed. Must be the lake. (*tenderly*) But what can I do, my poor sweetheart? What can I do?

Act Two

Dining room, just before lunch.

Arkádina (*to Masha*) Come on—on your feet.

They both stand.

Closer.
   Right—you're twenty-two and I'm nearly twice that. Evgenyi—who looks younger?

Dorn You. Obviously.

Arkádina Exactly—like a little bird. I could play a fifteen-year-old. The reason? I work—I travel—I participate—while you're always glued to your seat—you don't have a life. My rule is, don't try seeing ahead. I refuse to contemplate growing old—or dying. The future will happen when it happens.

Masha But I feel like I was born years and years ago. I'm dragging my life behind me like some kind of never-ending dress. Often I don't even *want* a life. (*She sits back down.*) Yes yes—I'm talking rubbish. 'Pull yourself together.' 'Get over it.'

Dorn begins to hum.
   Sorin comes on using a stick, Nina next to him, carrying a bunch of flowers. Medviedenko behind them pushes an empty wheelchair.

Sorin (*as if talking about a child*) Well well—take a look at this (*i.e., Nina*) —our father and stepmother have gone away, and we have three whole days of freedom.

Nina I'm so happy. I'm completely in your hands.

22

Sorin (*sits in the wheelchair*) And looking so very pretty today.

Arkádina Nicely dressed . . . not unattractive . . . and very very sweet. (*Kisses Nina.*) Where's Aleksei?

Nina Down by the swimming hut—fishing.

Arkádina He must be bored out of his brain.

Nina What is it you're reading?

Arkádina Maupassant. About writers. He says a woman inviting a writer into her house is like a miller inviting a rat into the granary. (*She shuts the book.*) Can someone please please tell me what's got into my son? Why's he being so horrid and depressed? He's out on that lake all day long and I hardly ever see him.

Masha He's unhappy. (*to Nina*) Please would you do us a bit of his play?

Nina Really? It's so boring.

Masha Not when *he* does it—when he reads it himself somehow it comes alive—don't you think? And his voice makes it so sad and beautiful.

   Sorin's snoring audible.

Dorn Sweet dreams.

Arkádina Petrúsha!

Sorin Mmm?

Arkádina Are you asleep?

Sorin Not remotely.

   Pause.

Arkádina You won't take your medication—that's the problem.

Sorin I'd be happy to take my medication but the doctor here says it's not worth prescribing.

Dorn Medication? At sixty?

Sorin I still want to live.

Dorn (*cross*) Fine. Take vitamins.

Arkádina *I* think he'd benefit from going to Baden-Baden, don't you?

Dorn Well, he might benefit from going to Baden-Baden—or of course he might not.

Arkádina Meaning?

Dorn Meaning nothing. Meaning just that.

Pause.

Medviedenko *I* think your brother should give up smoking.

Sorin Rubbish.

Dorn Not rubbish at all. Drinking and smoking alter people's personalities. It's like Jekyll and Hyde. And I can tell you, I've been on pretty intimate terms with both.

Sorin (*laughs*) Very good. Spoken like a real man of the world. Like a man who's really lived and not spent twenty-eight years of his life like me stagnating in a government department. You've seen it all already—good for you—but I've seen precisely nothing and consequently want a life, and if that means smoking cigars and having a few drinks or whatever with my dinner then to hell with it.

Dorn Life's to be lived, yes—but for a sixty-year-old man to imagine I can write a prescription that's going to compensate for his wasted youth is—well I'm sorry, but it's a joke.

Masha (*stands*) I'll see what's happening in the kitchen. (*Moves away, dragging her leg.*) My leg's gone dead . . . (*Goes out.*)

Dorn She's off for her two shots before lunch.

Sorin Poor child—she's so deeply unhappy.

Dorn With respect: that's rubbish.

Sorin You say that because you've / already *lived*.

Arkádina Country boredom is so uniquely and charmingly boring, don't you think? Hot—quiet— nothing to do—everyone picking away at things . . . Friends, friends, I do enjoy your company—don't get me wrong—but sitting in a hotel room learning a part— nothing beats that.

Nina (*with enthusiasm*) Absolutely. I completely understand.

Sorin Well, of course it's better in town—you've got telephones . . . cabs out in the street . . . whatever.

Dorn begins to hum.

Shamraev comes in, followed by Polina.

Shamraev Here they all are. Good morning good morning. (*Kisses Arkádina's hand, then Nina's.*) And looking so well. (*to Arkádina*) My wife tells me the two of you were planning to go into the town this afternoon, is that right?

Arkádina Planning to—yes.

Shamraev Hmm . . . excellent. But—with respect—how were you intending to get there? We're moving the rye— all the men are busy—and precisely which horses did you imagine you could take?

Arkádina Which horses? How do *I* know which horses?

Sorin The carriage horses.

Shamraev (*agitated*) The carriage horses? And how exactly am I supposed to tack them up? Mmm? How exactly do I tack them up? Amazing. Unbelievable. With respect: forgive me, because I admire your talent and would willingly give you ten years of my life—but horses: not possible.

Arkádina But what if I *have* to go? Most odd.

Shamraev I'm sorry, but I'm actually trying to run a farm here.

Arkádina (*flaring up*) Same old story. Well in that case I'm going straight back to Moscow. Either hire me some horses from the village or I'm walking to the station.

Shamraev (*flaring up*) Well in that case I resign. Find yourself another manager. (*Goes out.*)

Arkádina Every summer's the same—every summer here they humiliate me. I'm going and this time I won't be coming back. (*Goes out.*)

Sorin (*flaring up*) Jesus Christ. What the hell gets into him? I'm totally sick of this. I WANT EVERY HORSE HERE NOW.

Nina (*to Polina*) How can he say that to Irina Arkádina? Whatever she wants it's more important than running a stupid farm.

Polina (*in despair*) What can I do? Put yourself in my position—what can I do?

Arkádina brings Trigorin with his fishing rods through the room and off into another part of the house.

Sorin (*to Nina*) Let's go and talk to her . . . We'll all beg her not to leave. Agreed? (*looking to where Shamraev went out*) Revolting man. Bully.

Nina (*restraining him*) Sit still, sit still, we'll take you.

She and Medviedenko wheel the wheelchair.

This is so *awful* . . .

Sorin Yes yes, awful . . . But he won't resign—I'll talk to him.

They go out. Dorn and Polina remain.

Dorn God, the way they behave. They should've kicked out your darling husband years ago, but of course it will end up with that old fool in the wheelchair and his sister begging for his forgiveness. Typical.

Polina And what he *didn't* say, was he's got the carriage horses out in the fields as *well*. He's so bloody stupid and pig-headed. Why does it always have to be like this? Day after day after day of it.

Evgenyi—please—just get me away from here. And our poor Masha . . . Life's nearly over. Please. Can't we just tell everyone the truth?

Pause.

Dorn I'm fifty-five. It's too late.

Polina I know you're saying that because there's not just me, there are other women as well. I do understand. But you can't live with all of them.

I'm sorry: I know I'm boring.

Dorn No—not at all.

Polina I'm so jealous. But you can't avoid women— obviously—it's your job. I do understand.

Nina enters.

Dorn (*to Nina*) How's things?

Nina Irina's crying and her brother's having an asthma attack. It's so weird—isn't it—to see a famous actress crying . . . and for no reason.

Dorn I'd better go in.

Nina (*hands him flowers*) For you.

Dorn Thank you—*mademoiselle*.

Polina What exquisite flowers.

> *Dorn and Polina head for the room where Arkádina is.*

(*low and intense*) Give me those flowers. I said give me those flowers. (*On getting the flowers, she tears them to pieces and throws them onto the floor.*)

> *Dorn goes in to find Arkádina, and Polina leaves another way.*

> *Konstantin enters from the garden with a rifle and a dead seagull.*

Konstantin Are you alone?

Nina Yes. Why? What does this mean?

Konstantin I was sick-minded enough today to kill this gull. I place it before you.

> *He puts it on the dining table.*

Nina What's wrong with you?

Konstantin (*pause*) Soon I shall kill myself in the same way.

Nina You're not making any sense.

Konstantin Well neither are you. Look at you. You'd rather I wasn't here.

Nina Stop being so angry. Why d'you have to make everything so . . . incredibly complicated? This is obviously meant to be some kind of symbol—but I'm sorry, I don't see it. I must just be too stupid to see it.

Konstantin I burnt my play. I thought you'd like to know. (*She looks at him.*) I cannot believe that you are behaving like this. It's like waking up and seeing this lake evaporate—or drain away into the earth.

Trigorin enters.

You're not stupid. Don't pretend. (*Goes quickly out into the garden.*)

Nina Hello.

Trigorin Hello. (*faint laugh*) What's this?

Nina A seagull. Konstantin killed it.

Trigorin It's . . . extraordinary. (*Pause.*) Well. Seems we have to leave. So we're unlikely to meet again. Sadly. I don't often get to meet young women—I mean young *and* interesting—and I've completely forgotten what it's like being only eighteen or nineteen—which is why the girls in my stories are never quite real. I'd love to spend just one hour being you so I could get inside that little head of yours and find out what really goes on in there.

Nina Well I'd like to be *you*.

Trigorin Why's that?

Nina To know what it feels like being a famous writer. What makes you most aware of it?

Trigorin Aware of it? Nothing. I've never thought about it. (*Reflects.*) Hmm . . . either you're making me out more famous than I really am or fame's not something I'm ever aware of.

Nina But surely when you read about yourself in the papers . . .

Trigorin It's great when it's good—and when it's bad, for a couple of days I get depressed.

Nina But it's a different universe. You've no idea how jealous I am. Most of us just drag ourselves through lives of total monotony—everyone the same—everyone unhappy. While people like you—the one in a million like you—lead brilliant fascinating lives that actually *mean* something. And make you happy.

Trigorin Me? (*Shrugs.*) I'm sorry, but words like brilliant and famous and fascinating are—forgive me—like the kind of sticky pudding I never eat. You are very young and very kind.

Nina That doesn't mean you have to condescend to me.

Trigorin Oh really? Fine then. Listen. D'you know what a 'fixed idea' is?—like when someone obsesses about . . . God knows what . . . the moon? Well my moon, my single obsessive thought, is writing. Write write write— it's a compulsion. I finish one story and for whatever reason straight away I'm forced to begin the next—and the next, and the next, and the next—on and on and on and on endlessly—that's how it is. Brilliant and meaningful? Obsessive-compulsive, more like it. Here I am for example talking to you now—genuinely talking— but at the same time I know there's always a story lurking. I see a cloud, for instance—one like a grand piano—and I'm thinking, I must get that cloud like a grand piano into my story. Or I smell the jasmine and I think: 'jasmine—white stars—heavy scent—use to describe summer evening.' Every word that you or I are saying now is being spiked on a pin and stored in a special box marked literature. And even when I stop working and drag myself off to the theatre, or out fishing, to forget, to empty my mind, I can't: there's this great steel ball rolling round my skull—new idea!—back to the desk!—write write write! That's how it is—that's how it always is—no peace—not even from myself. I don't have a life, you see—just raw material.

Nina But surely writing and being creative gives you an incredible feeling.

Trigorin Yes. Writing's very nice. And reading the proofs is nice. But as soon as the stuff comes out in print I hate it—I see all the faults—it's a mistake—a mistake to 've even written it—which is when all the self-loathing starts. (*Laughs.*) And people go: 'Yes very competent, but Turgenev's better' or 'Very accomplished writing, but it's hardly *War and Peace*'. And I will go on being 'accomplished' and 'competent' and failing to write *War and Peace* until the day I die.

Nina I'm sorry but you're not making sense. You've been spoilt by your success.

Trigorin Success? Writing is one long self-punishment, I'm afraid. It would be fine if you could spend your whole life just describing landscapes—water for example, trees, the sky—the things I can write about almost instinctively. But the fact is, writers have responsibilities—we can't not engage—we're expected to have views about things— science, social justice, human rights, women's rights— you name it—so that's what I do—go jumping from one set of issues to the next while all the time life itself—the one thing that really matters—moves further and further away—and I'm left standing on the platform watching it disappear—like the peasant who's missed his train.

Nina You're too close to what you do. Just because you're so self-critical doesn't mean you're not a great writer.

Trigorin A great writer? What? Like Shakespeare?

They both smile. Pause.

Nina If I was lucky enough to be able to write or act I'd put up with any amount of poverty or disappointment or disapproval from my family. I'd live in just one room and only eat bread and of course I'd be self-critical and aware of all my faults but in return I'd have to be famous—totally incredibly famous . . . (*Covers her face with her hands.*) I'm losing my balance . . . weird . . .

Arkádina (*calls, off*) Aleksei?

Trigorin I'm wanted.
    Don't really feel like leaving. (*Looks out at the lake.*) It's truly special here. Amazing.

Nina You know the house and garden on the other side?

Trigorin Yes.

Nina It was my mother's when she was alive. I was born there. I've spent my whole life by this lake and I know every tiny island.

Trigorin Wonderful place to live. (*Slight pause.*) Hmm.

Nina What?

Trigorin Nothing. Just an idea—an idea for a story. Young girl lives on shore of lake since childhood—like you. Loves the lake—like the seagull. Is happy and free—like the seagull. Then one day a man turns up, sees her, and mindlessly destroys her—just like this seagull.

   Pause. Arkádina enters.

Arkádina Aleksei?

Trigorin What is it?

Arkádina We're staying.

   Trigorin follows Arkádina back into the room.

Nina It's a dream.

Act Three

*A corridor in the house. Early morning. Signs of
preparation for departure. Trigorin and Masha.*

Masha Look—you're a writer—so you can put this in
one of your novels. If he'd really done it—killed
himself—I honestly couldn't've gone on living. But as it
is, I've made up my mind. My plan is to cut love right
out of me.

Trigorin How?

Masha Get married. To Semyon.

Trigorin What? The schoolteacher?

Masha Yes.

Trigorin And the point?

Masha The point? The point is I stop waiting for
something that will never happen. Get married and I
won't even have time to think about it. Love, I mean.
Too many responsibilities—make a nice change. Top up?

Trigorin Is that wise?

Masha Oh spare me. (*Pours out drinks.*) And don't look
at me like that. You think women don't drink? Of course
they do—only most of them do it in secret. Oh yes.
Vodka and brandy. (*Clinks glasses.*) Cheers. I'm going
to miss you.

Trigorin Well, I'm going to miss being here.

Masha Then make her stay.

Trigorin She won't. Not after what's happened.

Pause.

Nina comes into the corridor.

Masha Well. Look. I wish you all the very best. Please don't think I'm a bad person. (*Shakes his hand warmly.*) It was very kind of you to listen. I'll expect a signed copy of your next book. And you can put: 'For Masha—no idea where she comes from—no idea what she's living for.' Goodbye. (*Goes out.*)

Nina (*stretching out her clenched fist*) Odd or even?

Trigorin Even.

Nina Wrong. Look: just one pea. If you'd said odd, it would've meant be an actress. I don't know what to do—I need advice.

Trigorin It's not possible to give advice.

Pause.

Nina Listen . . . You're leaving and I may never see you again . . . (*Produces a book.*) It's one of yours—*When Day Turns to Night*—I want you to write in it for me.

Trigorin Of course. I'd love to. What shall I put?

Nina (*stopping him opening the book*) Not now please. Later. When you've looked in it.

Trigorin Oh? (*Slight pause.*) Alright. Later then.

Nina Think of me sometimes.

Trigorin Of course I will. I'll think how you looked in the sunlight—remember?—last week—in that wonderful dress. We were both talking . . . and there was a white gull.

Nina Yes . . . the seagull.

Pause.

Arkádina (*off*) You ought to be staying indoors. You're not well enough to go socialising.

Nina There's somebody coming. Remember the book. You're not to leave without seeing me.

Nina goes out as Arkádina and Sorin come in, Sorin dressed to go somewhere. Yakov deals with the packing.

Arkádina (*to Trigorin*) Who was that? Nina?

Trigorin Yes. (*He starts to leaf through the book.*)

Arkádina Well I'm sorry if we disturbed you.

Yakov (*to Trigorin*) You want me to pack the fishing rods?

Trigorin has stopped at a particular page of the book, and is engrossed by it.

Arkádina Aleksei?

Trigorin What?

Arkádina He asked you a question—the fishing rods.

Trigorin Yes. Fine. Pack them. (*He moves away, preoccupied.*) But not the books. You can give them away. (*Goes out.*)

Arkádina I'm serious, Petrúsha—you stay here in the house.

Sorin I don't want to be left here on my own.

Arkádina But why go into the town?

Sorin No reason. God knows. (*Laughs.*) Watch local government in action? Whatever. The horses will be here in fifteen minutes. We can leave at the same time.

Arkádina (*after a pause*) Well. Don't get too bored. Don't catch cold. And keep your eye on Konstantin. Take care of him. Sort him out.

Pause.

Why did he *do* that to himself?

Sorin Look. How can I put this? He's young, he's bright, he's stuck out here in the country, got no money, no status, and no future. Now I love the boy enormously and he's very attached to me—but at the same time he knows he's redundant here, and is basically—well—scrounging.

Arkádina (*not listening*) He really worries me. Perhaps we should find him a job . . .

Sorin (*whistles, then*) Well. Hmm. The best thing . . . might be if you gave him a little money. I'd say some new clothes would make a major difference. He's had on the same old jacket now for the past three years—and he's no winter coat. (*Laughs.*) Wouldn't hurt him to enjoy life either—would it?—travel?—do Europe?—whatever—wouldn't cost the earth.

Arkádina Well. Yes. Maybe some new clothes—but as for Europe . . . No. I can't. Not even clothes—I don't have the money.

Sorin laughs.

I don't.

Sorin (*whistles*) Of course not. Forgive me—don't be angry—I believe you. You're always exceptionally kind and generous.

Arkádina I DON'T HAVE THE MONEY.

Sorin If I had money, well obviously, I'd pay for him myself, no questions asked, but I've got nothing, not one

36

penny. (*Laughs.*) All of my pension goes straight to Ilya who then proceeds to experiment with his cattle-breeding or bee-keeping or whatever it is—and that's the last I ever see of it. The bees die, the cows die—and the horses are / never available.

Arkádina Well of course I've got *some* money, but there's my work—you know we have to pay for everything—even our own costumes.

Sorin You're very kind. And very good. Of course you are . . . Of course you are . . . (*He sways.*) Ah . . . (*He grips the table.*)

Arkádina (*frightened*) Petrúsha? (*Tries to hold him up.*) Petrúsha—come on—stand up. (*Shouts.*) WILL SOMEBODY PLEASE HELP ME.

> *Konstantin comes in with a bandage round his head, followed by Medviedenko.*

He looked like he was going to collapse.

Sorin Nonsense . . . nonsense . . . (*Smiles and drinks some water.*) You see: totally recovered.

Konstantin (*to Arkádina*) This is what he does now—it's nothing—we're used to it. (*to Sorin*) Aren't we? Yes? You need a little lie-down, don't you?

Sorin Yes, just a little one. But I'm still going into town. A little lie-down, then I'm off. No questions asked. (*He moves off, using his stick.*)

Medviedenko (*taking his arm*) Remember that riddle? On four legs in the morning, on two at noon, and in the evening on three.

Sorin (*laughing*) And night-time flat on his back—don't remind me. Please. I can manage on my own.

Medviedenko No—come on—let me help.

He and Sorin go out.

Arkádina He had me terrified.

Konstantin Living out here isn't good for him. It makes him fret. On the other hand if you suddenly went mad and lent him—what?—twenty thousand?—he could start living in town.

Arkádina I have no money. I'm an actress, not a banker.

Pause.

Konstantin Will you change my bandage? You're really good at it.

Arkádina The doctor's late.

Konstantin He promised to be here by eight and it's nearly eleven o'clock.

Arkádina Sit down. (*Takes off his bandage.*) You do look funny. Like a cross between a wounded soldier and an Egyptian mummy. There. Almost completely healed. Just scratches really. (*Kisses his head.*) No more silly guns when I've gone—mmm?

Konstantin Of course not. It was stupid—I lost control. Won't happen again. (*Kisses her hands.*) Your hands are so magic. Remember—ages ago—you were starting out, and I was still tiny—remember that fight in our building when that laundrywoman got seriously injured? She had to be carried back to her room? And you visited her every day—took her medicine—washed her children in an old metal bath? You must remember.

Arkádina No. (*Puts on new bandage.*)

Konstantin Then there were the two ballet-dancers living upstairs? They used to come in for coffee?

Arkádina Them I remember.

Konstantin Both really religious?

Pause.

Just recently—these last few days—I've started loving
you without even thinking about it—just like when I was
little. Apart from you, I've nobody left. But why is it?—
why is it you let that man control you?

Arkádina You don't understand him, Konstantin.
Morally, he's scrupulous.

Konstantin Oh yes, so scrupulous that when he finds out
I want to challenge him, he ups and leaves.

Arkádina Rubbish. It's *me making* him leave. Listen,
I don't expect you to approve of our relationship, but
you're intelligent and civilised and I'm entitled to ask
you to respect my freedom.

Konstantin I'll respect your freedom if you'll respect
mine, which means letting me have an opinion. Morally
scrupulous? He's got the two of us at each other's
throats and at the same time he's in this house salivating
over Nina and trying to convince her he's a genius.

Arkádina You obviously enjoy hurting my feelings.
I respect that man and I will not hear him abused.

Konstantin Well I don't. You'd like me to believe he's
a genius as well, but I'm sorry, his writing makes me
vomit.

Arkádina You're jealous. People with no talent always
try and belittle the ones with real talent—just like your
father did.

Konstantin Real talent? (*with anger*) I've got more talent
than all of them put together. (*Pulls off the bandage.*)
It's you—the reactionaries—who grab the positions of
power, decide what is or is not art, and suffocate the rest

of us. I refuse to recognise your authority. And I refuse to recognise his.

Arkádina Oh grow up.

Konstantin Go back to your precious theatre and carry on doing your banal little dramas.

Arkádina I have never done anything banal. How dare you. You can't even write one convincing scene—just lounge about here scrounging off my brother. It's sick.

Konstantin Tight-fisted bitch.

Arkádina Parasite.

Konstantin sits down and quietly cries.

Nonentity.

Pause.

Don't cry. Please don't cry. (*She cries.*) Please—you're not to. (*Kisses his forehead, his cheeks, his head.*) Sweetheart . . . Forgive me . . . I'm a bad person . . . I'm sorry.

Konstantin (*embraces her*) You don't realise. I've got nothing. She doesn't love me and I can't write any more . . . It's hopeless.

Arkádina Come on. Don't give up. Things will sort out. He's leaving, and she'll fall back in love with you. (*Wipes his tears.*) She will—alright? Friends?

Konstantin (*kisses her hands*) Yes. Of course.

Arkádina (*gently*) And you're to be friends with him too. No need for fighting. Is there?

Konstantin Alright. But please—I don't want to have to see him. It's too painful . . . I don't have the energy.

Trigorin comes into the corridor.

I'm going to go. The doctor can do this later.

Konstantin picks the bandage off the floor and goes.

Arkádina (*looking at watch*) They'll soon be round with the horses.

Pause.

I assume you've packed?

Trigorin Of course I have. Listen—let's stay for one more day.

Arkádina shakes her head.

One more day. Why not?

Arkádina Because—sweetheart—I know exactly what you're after. So control yourself. You've been drinking—try and act like a grown-up.

Trigorin Then you be a grown-up too. It's not like we've locked ourselves into some kind of stereotypical marriage. Mmm?

Arkádina Just what is it, Aleksei, you are trying to / say to me?

Trigorin And this could be exactly what I need.

Arkádina What you need? Going to bed with some clueless little child is 'what you need'? You have / *no idea*.

Trigorin Because there is this image in my head—we're having this conversation but at the same time there is this image of her in my head and I can't get rid of it.

Arkádina Don't want to get rid of it is what you mean. *You cannot talk to me like this, Aleksei.* I am a normal person and I have / normal feelings.

Trigorin Of course you are, of course you are. But imagine waking up and she's next to you—she's right there—her head's right there on the pillow and she's looking straight into your eyes—completely open—totally trusting—and it's like she's taken you back to the exact point in your life where everything was possible but you failed to realise. You had the capacity to love but were simply too young / to realise.

Arkádina I DO NOT WANT TO HEAR THIS.

Trigorin LET ME.

Arkádina Why is everybody today so determined to / undermine me.

Trigorin You don't understand. You don't *want* / to understand.

Arkádina Am I really so old and ugly that I have to stand here and listen to you fantasise about that girl?

Embraces and kisses him.

Come on come on come on, this isn't serious—you can't be serious—she's just a child—some silly little child who thinks she can act, mmm? (*Clings to him.*) Because you know what would happen if you left me—don't you—mmm?—don't you—you know I wouldn't last five minutes without you—don't you—you know I'd die—don't you—don't you—hurt myself—kill myself—yes?

Trigorin (*trying to get her off*) Someone will see.

Arkádina Why shouldn't they see? Why shouldn't they see how much I love you? Poor darling—you've got obsessed—you're obsessed and you want to do something stupid but don't worry: I'm not going to let you. Because I know what you're like—I know how you get obsessed—I know you so well—don't I—mmm? And your writing—mmm? Always so clear, and direct, and funny, and surprising. The way just a tiny detail makes a whole person or a whole landscape come alive—yes? Truly great. Look at my eyes. Come on. Look. *Look at me.* (*Forces him to meet her eyes.*) You see. *Truly great.* Truly the one great writer of your generation and there is nobody else—no child—no stupid little child—mmm?— mmm?—who could ever appreciate or understand that truth as deeply or as passionately as I do.

Pause.

Trigorin (*inaudible*) I'll come.

Arkádina What?

Trigorin (*audible*) I said alright—I'll come.

Arkádina (*as if nothing had happened*) But of course if you want to stay on then let's stay on. Or I'll go today, and you come . . . whenever you like—sometime next week if you'd rather.

Trigorin No. I'll come today.

Arkádina Because what you do is completely your decision.

Pause. Trigorin takes out his notebook.

What is it?

Trigorin Just this thing somebody said today. 'The forest looks angry.' (*Repeats the phrase as he writes it in his book.*) 'The forest . . . looks . . . angry.' Not bad. (*He closes the book and stretches.*) Well that's it then— railway stations, railway trains, railway food and railway conversations.

Shamraev (*enters*) Don't want to disturb you but—with respect—the horses are ready. Time to leave for the station. Train goes at five past twelve. (*to Arkádina*) Oh, and you won't forget, will you, to ask about Semenov?

43

That's assuming he's still alive. We used to go drinking together. He was amazing in *Murder in Minsk*—him and Kanatchikov—now he was a character—where was it?— I know: Petersburg. Really—there's no panic—we've still got five minutes. Anyway, the two of them were in this thriller—playing subversives—and when they got caught they had to say: 'We repent. We acknowledge the Tsar'— only Kanatchikov goes: 'We abolish the Tsar.' (*Roars with laughter.*) 'Abolish the Tsar.'

> *During the preceding, Yakov sorts out the luggage, a Maid brings Arkádina's coat, umbrella and gloves, and everyone helps her put them on. The (male) Cook first peeps in, then enters. In comes Polina, followed by Sorin and Medviedenko.*

Polina (*with a basket*) I've brought you some plums . . . nice sweet ones. Thought you might like them for the journey.

Arkádina That's very kind of you, Polina.

Polina Do take care. And I'm sorry if things haven't been . . . as they should've been. (*Begins to cry.*)

Arkádina (*embraces her*) Everything's been marvellous. Come on: no need to cry.

Polina Time goes by so fast.

Arkádina No use complaining.

Sorin (*dressed to go out, with stick*) We should go or you'll end up missing the train. I'll be outside . . . (*Goes out.*)

Medviedenko I'm going to walk. If I hurry I can see you off from the station . . . (*Goes out.*)

Arkádina My dear dear friends—goodbye . . . goodbye. Until next summer—with any luck.

The Maid, Yakov and the Cook kiss her hand.

Don't forget me. (*Gives Cook money.*) This is for the three of you.

Cook Thank you. Have a good journey. Much appreciated.

Yakov You take care of yourself.

Shamraev Please write to us, won't you? (*to Trigorin*) Goodbye. Have a / good trip.

Arkádina Where's Konstantin? Tell him I'm leaving. We need to say goodbye. Well . . . think of me—yes? (*to Yakov*) I've given something to the cook. It's for you three to share.

They all go. Sound of people being seen off. The Maid comes back to get the basket of plums and goes out again. Trigorin then comes in looking for something. Nina enters.

Trigorin Ah. Forgot my rods. We were just leaving.

Nina And I came to get my book back. Weird.

Pause.

Trigorin The thing you wrote in it . . . did you mean that?

Nina Why wouldn't I mean it? Listen—Aleksei—I've made up my mind about acting. I'm leaving—leaving home, leaving my father—I'm coming to Moscow.
How do I find you?

Trigorin (*glancing behind him*) D'you know the Hotel Rubliev?

Nina shakes her head. He gets out his notebook and draws her a map.

I'll show you. Look. This is the station . . . and this . . . is Boulevard Malinowski . . . and here—look—is the hotel.

Gives her the map.

Check into a room and wait. I have to go.

Pause.

Nina Stay one more minute.

Trigorin I can't.

He goes.

Two years elapse before the following act.

Act Four

*The dining room in Sorin's house, now turned into a
study for Konstantin. A writing table. The grand piano
from Act One. Evening. Sound of wind and trees, and
of the watchman's rattle. One lamp is on. Masha can be
heard calling 'Konstantin? Konstantin?'*

Medviedenko and Masha enter.

Masha Konstantin?
  He's vanished. The old man keeps going 'Where's
Kostya? Where's Kostya?'

Medviedenko He's afraid of being alone. (*Listens.*) What
horrible weather. Two days it's been like this.

Masha (*turns on another lamp*) There're waves on the
lake. Huge ones.

Medviedenko The garden's so dark. We should've got
them to take down that theatre. It's like a skeleton—and
the curtains won't stop flapping. Yesterday evening I
thought I could hear someone behind it—crying.

Masha Behind it?

  Pause.

Medviedenko Masha—let's go home.

Masha (*shakes head*) I'm spending the night here.

Medviedenko Please. He'll be hungry.

Masha Rubbish. Sophie will feed him.

  Pause.

Medviedenko That's three nights now you haven't been there.

Masha God you're pathetic. Sometimes you at least used to express an opinion—now it's all baby this, baby that—baby baby baby, I'm sick of it.

Medviedenko Please.

Masha You go.

Medviedenko Your father won't give me any horses.

Masha Yes he will. Just go and ask.

Medviedenko Then you'll come back tomorrow?

Masha (*lights cigarette*) Alright—tomorrow—nag nag nag.

Enter Konstantin and Polina.

Polina Found him.

Konstantin goes to his table and sits. Polina follows him and looks at his writing.

Pause.

Medviedenko Well. I'm going. Goodbye Masha. (*Kisses her.*) Goodbye Polina. (*Tries to kiss her.*)

Polina (*dismissive*) Yes yes yes—safe journey.

Medviedenko Goodbye Konstantin.

Konstantin Goodbye.

Medviedenko goes out.

Polina (*looking at Konstantin's writing*) Whoever would've thought you'd turn into a real writer . . . Stories in magazines . . . Cheques in the post . . . (*Runs her hand through his hair.*) Not bad-looking these days either. Kostya—sweetheart—try and be a bit more friendly with my poor Masha.

Masha Please. Leave it.

Polina She's a sweet little thing.

Pause.

All a woman wants, Kostya, is the occasional friendly glance. I should know.

Konstantin gets up and walks out.

Masha Now he's angry. Why can't you keep your mouth shut.

Polina I feel sorry for you, sweetheart.

Masha Great help that is.

Polina I know exactly what you're going through and it breaks my heart.

Masha Lovesick women only exist in novels. It's all rubbish. I'm not going to spend my life wasting away like some stupid princess in a tower.

Konstantin comes back in.

As soon as Semyon gets his transfer, we're leaving—end of story.

Konstantin begins to play the piano. After a moment Masha begins dancing to the music. Then Medviedenko can be heard.

Medviedenko (*off*) So of course what with my mother, and Sophie, you can see how tight things are . . .

Enter Dorn and Medviedenko pushing Sorin in the wheelchair.

. . . More than six people to feed. And half my salary going just on bread.

Dorn Well you've still got the other half.

Medviedenko Very funny. But of course you've got money to burn.

Dorn Money? I'll tell you something: in thirty years as a doctor—and that's thirty punishing years of being constantly on call—the most I've ever saved is twenty thousand—and I've just blown all that travelling. I've got absolutely nothing.

Masha (*to Medviedenko*) I thought you were going.

Medviedenko I can't. He won't let me have a horse.

Masha Christ why don't you just piss off?

Pause.

Dorn Well . . . it's all completely different. You've turned this dining room into a study.

Masha Konstantin prefers it for working. He can use the garden when he wants to think.

Sound of watchman.

Sorin Where's my sister?

Dorn Gone to the station to meet Aleksei. She won't be long.

Sorin The way you've all summoned her here, I'm assuming I'm dangerously ill.

Silence.

I'm dangerously ill but no one will prescribe me anything.

Dorn What would you like me to prescribe? Vitamins? Cod-liver oil?

Sorin Don't start all that again. Life's punishment enough. Not here then.

Polina Not yet.

Dorn hums softly and continues as Sorin speaks.

Sorin I've got an idea for one of Konstantin's stories. The title is—'The Man Who Did Not'. When I was young I wanted to become a writer—but I Did Not. I wanted to speak intelligently—and did I speak intelligently?—no I Did Not. (*Parodies himself.*) 'From which we can infer whatever whatever no questions asked blah blah blah.' Even in court I went on like that till it felt like my brain was sticking to my skull. I wanted to get married but of course I Did Not. I was desperate to live in a town—but now look at me: stuck here in the country rotting to death.

Dorn 'I wanted to be a Senior Civil Servant with a fat pension and I succeeded.'

Sorin (*laughs*) Yes—but that wasn't an ambition—it just happened.

Dorn Come on—you're an old man—stop complaining: it sounds so petty.

Sorin It's not petty to want a life.

Dorn You've *had* a life. But life ends. It's normal.

Sorin You say that because you've done things. You've done things with your life so you don't care any more. But even you'll find death frightening.

Dorn Fear of death is completely irrational—unless you're religious and think you'll get punished for your sins. But in your case (a), you're not exactly religious— and (b), you've committed no sins—unless we count twenty-five years as a civil servant.

Sorin (*laughs*) Twenty-eight.

Enter Konstantin.

Dorn We're stopping Konstantin from working.

Konstantin Doesn't matter.

Pause.

Medviedenko I was wondering—Doctor—which was your favourite foreign city.

Dorn Genoa.

Konstantin Why Genoa?

Dorn It's the amazingly crowded streets. You come out of your hotel in the evening and the whole street's seething with people. You just get swept along—but nowhere in particular—you're just moving with the crowd—like you're all part of the same thought. Or like that speech Nina did in your play—'heartbeat of the world' or something. (*Slight pause.*) What happened to her exactly?

Konstantin Nina? I'm sure she's fine.

Dorn I heard her life got a bit chaotic. Is that true?

Konstantin It's a long story.

Dorn Well shorten it.

Pause.

Konstantin After she ran away she began seeing Aleksei Trigorin. You knew that.

Dorn Yes.

Konstantin She had a baby. The baby died. Trigorin left her and resumed his previous . . . relationship. As you would expect. In fact he'd never really given it up but somehow . . . revoltingly . . . juggled them both. So . . . as I understand it, her emotional life has been . . . well, fairly disastrous.

Dorn And acting?

Konstantin Even worse, apparently. She started off with some kind of semi-professional outfit outside of Moscow, then went on tour. I . . . followed her in fact and . . . well I watched what she did. She got big parts—but her acting was really crude—too much shouting and arm-waving. Once or twice she'd do something real—something truly electric—but only once or twice.

Dorn So she has got talent.

Konstantin (*faint laugh*) Yes—probably—who knows. Anyway—she totally refused to see me.

Pause.

What else can I say? I got back here and sometimes she'd write to me. She was lucid—generous—never complained. But she started signing herself 'Seagull'. And that's what she kept on calling herself in her letters. Now she's here.

Dorn What d'you mean: now she's here?

Konstantin Here in the town. In a hotel. She's been there five days. I've tried going—and so very kindly has Masha—but she won't see anyone. Semyon says he met her yesterday afternoon in a field about a mile from here.

Medviedenko That's right. She was heading towards the town. I said hello and asked her why she hadn't come to visit. She said she would.

Konstantin She won't.

Pause.

Her father and stepmother have actually hired people to keep her off their property.

He goes with Dorn to the writing table.

It's one thing sorting life out on paper, but something else to do it in reality.

Sorin She was entirely gorgeous.

Dorn I'm sorry? Say / that again?

Sorin I said she was entirely gorgeous. Used to have quite a thing about her once.

Dorn You old lecher.

Polina Sounds like they're back from the station.

Konstantin Yes—that's my mother.

Arkádina (*off*) Age? What's age got to do with it?

Shamraev (*off, laughs*) With respect: everything, if you ask me.

Arkádina (*off*) I've really no idea what you mean.

Enter Arkádina, Trigorin, followed by Shamraev.

Shamraev What I mean is is while the rest of us get old—get ground down by the elements—you're just as young as ever . . . Went dancing down that platform like a teenage girl.

Arkádina (*flattered*) Teenage girl rubbish. I don't believe a / word of it.

Trigorin (*to Sorin*) Hello there. Bearing up? Excellent. (*with joy*) Masha!

Masha You recognised me. (*Shakes his hand.*)

Trigorin Married?

Masha Ages ago.

Trigorin Happy? (*to Dorn*) Nice to see you. (*to Medviedenko*) Hello again. (*Tentatively goes up to Konstantin.*) Irina says you've stopped being angry with me.

Konstantin offers his hand. Trigorin shakes it.

Arkádina Aleksei's brought the magazine with your new story in it.

Konstantin (*taking the journal, to Trigorin*) Thank you. That's very kind.

Trigorin I bring you best wishes from your adoring fans. You've made quite a stir in Petersburg and Moscow and I'm always being pestered about you—'What's he like? How old is he? Is he good-looking?' For some reason they all assume you're middle-aged. And because of this pseudonym, you've managed to make yourself a true Man of Mystery.

Konstantin Are you staying long?

Trigorin No. Back to Moscow tomorrow in fact. No choice. Story to finish—then I've promised someone something for an anthology. Same old business in fact.

Pause.

Arkádina Why don't we get the Lotto out.

Trigorin I think this weather's got it in for me. The wind out there's appalling. If it's dropped by morning I'm going down to the lake to fish. And the other thing is I need to take a look at the garden—the place where you did your play—remember? I've been working on a new piece—just have to remind myself about / the location.

Masha (*to Shamraev*) Daddy. Semyon needs a horse. He needs to go home.

Shamraev (*mocking*) 'Daddy, he needs a horse.' (*hard*)

You know as well as I do the horses are worn out. They're only just back from the station.

Masha But you've got other ones.

Shamraev ignores her.

It's like talking to a / brick wall.

Medviedenko I'm fine, Masha. I can walk.

Polina *Walk?* In *this* weather? (*She sits at table.*) Come on everyone. / Let's start.

Medviedenko It only takes a couple of hours. I'll see you tomorrow then, yes? (*Kisses Masha, then to Polina.*) Goodnight Polina.

Polina reluctantly allows herself to be kissed.

I don't mean to cause any trouble—it's just the baby. So . . . (*looking round at them all*) Goodnight everyone. (*He leaves.*)

Shamraev He'll survive. It's not like he hasn't got legs.

Polina (*knocking on the table*) Come on, come on, hurry up or it'll be supper-time.

Shamraev, Masha and Dorn sit at the table.

Arkádina (*to Trigorin*) This is what we do here autumn evenings: play Lotto. D'you want to join in? One game before supper?

She sits at table with Trigorin and distributes the scorecards for the game.

Look: these are the same old cards we had when we were little and played it with our mother. It's totally boring but quite fun when you get the hang of it.

Konstantin is leafing through the journal.

What about you, Kostya?

Konstantin Mmm?

Arkádina Playing?

Konstantin Don't think so. Sorry.
(*coming over*) He's read his own story, but mine he hasn't even cut the pages.

Arkádina Shh shh shh . . . (*Kisses him on the head.*) Don't make such a fuss.

Konstantin puts the journal on his writing table and goes out.

Shamraev He's getting a lot of flak from the critics.

Arkádina He takes it all too seriously.

Trigorin He's unfortunate—he can't quite come up with an authentic voice. His work's weird—not quite in focus—autistic, almost. None of his characters are real.

Dorn Well I think he's got something—definitely got something. He thinks in pictures and those pictures of his get right under my skin. His only problem is is he doesn't know what to write about. But you must be very proud of him.

Arkádina Me? D'you know, I still haven't read a single word. There's never the time. (*Slight pause.*) Right. Usual stakes. Doctor—put mine in the kitty would you.

Dorn With pleasure.

Masha All put your money in? Here we go . . . (*She withdraws counters from the bag.*) Twenty-two.

Arkádina Me.

Masha Three.

Dorn That's mine.

Masha Done it? Seven. Eighty-one. Ten.

Shamraev Slow down a bit.

Konstantin comes back in.

Arkádina My God—that audience in Kharkov—complete insanity.

Masha Thirty-four.

Konstantin begins to play the piano.

Arkádina Not just seven calls but two minutes standing ovation . . . flowers landing on the stage . . . and even . . . (*Unfastens a piece of jewellery and tosses it onto the table.*) . . . look: sent to my dressing room.

Shamraev Very nice.

Masha Fifty.

Dorn Fifteen?

Masha Fifty—five-oh— / fifty.

Arkádina You should've seen me at the reception: say what you like, but I still know how / to wear clothes.

Polina Kostya. That sounds so sad.

Masha Eleven.

Arkádina (*glances at Sorin*) Petrúsha? Are you bored?

Pause.

He's asleep.

Dorn The sleep of a Senior Civil Servant.

Masha Seven. Ninety.

Trigorin If I lived on this kind of property—with a lake—I'm not sure I could be bothered to write. I suspect I'd concentrate on fishing.

Masha Twenty-eight.

Trigorin Ruff. Perch. Total bliss.

Masha Seventy-seven. Twenty-six.

Konstantin stops playing.

Shamraev (*to Trigorin*) Y'know we've been keeping that thing of yours, don't you.

Trigorin What thing?

Shamraev Konstantin shot that seagull and you asked me to have it stuffed.

Trigorin I don't remember. (*Thinks.*) I don't remember.

Konstantin flings open an outside door letting the air blast in.

Masha Sixty-six. One.

Arkádina Don't be so stupid, Kostya. Shut the door.

Konstantin shuts the door.

Masha Eighty-eight.

Trigorin Full house, my friends.

Arkádina (*with joy*) Brilliant, brilliant.

Shamraev Fantastic. Well done.

Arkádina This man is a born winner. (*Gets up.*) Let's eat shall we. Our poor star guest's had nothing since breakfast. We can carry on afterwards. (*to Konstantin*) Kostya, leave all that—come and eat something.

Konstantin No thanks. Not hungry.

Arkádina Suit yourself. (*Wakes Sorin.*) Petrúsha? Supper. (*Takes Shamraev's arm and moves off.*) Two whole minutes standing ovation . . .

Shamraev Incredible.

Arkádina . . . I thought those flowers would bury me alive. That's the thing about Kharkov . . . (*Goes out, continuing to speak.*) . . . they really appreciate what an actor can do—not everyone understands . . .

Shamraev (*off*) Absolutely.

Polina and Dorn push out the wheelchair.

Arkádina (*off*) . . . it's not just a profession, it's a vocation, you give it your whole life and it's only reasonable to expect something back . . .

All go out, leaving Konstantin alone.

He looks through his writing, and identifies a passage that needs work.

He crosses something out, and writes a new phrase.

He contemplates the new phrase.

He crosses out the new phrase, and writes an alternative.

He contemplates the alternative.

In disgust, he screws up the page.

Tapping on the window.

Konstantin Hello? Who is it?

Tapping again. He opens the window and looks out.

Hello?

He goes outside. He comes back with Nina. She's crying, but tries to suppress it.

(*very soft*) Hey hey hey—come on now—don't cry—shh shh shh shh—Nina . . . Nina . . . (*She moves away.*) I knew you'd come. I knew it. I've been thinking about it all day.

Nina There's somebody here.

Konstantin No. No one.

Nina What about your mother? Lock the doors.

Konstantin (*locks one door, but can't lock the other*) This one doesn't lock. (*He puts a chair in front of it.*) Alright? You see? No one can come in.

Nina Let me look at you. (*She looks intently at his face—then round the room.*) So warm in here. Nice. (*Slight pause.*) Do I look very different?

Konstantin Yes.

Nina Thinner?

Konstantin Mmm?

Nina How do I look different?

Konstantin I don't know. This is / too strange.

Nina Is it my eyes?

Konstantin I don't understand. Why wouldn't you see me? You've been here nearly a week. I keep going to that hotel, but they won't / let me in.

Nina I was frightened you hated me. I keep dreaming you're looking at me but you don't know who I am. You can't imagine what it's like . . . coming back here . . . walking by the lake. I've been close to your house lots of times, but didn't dare come in.

   Slight pause.

So warm in here. Nice. Snug. Listen to that wind. What's that thing in Turgenev? 'Happy the man, on nights such as these, snug in his own home.' I'm the seagull—is that right?—no. (*Rubs forehead.*) What was I saying? Oh yes. 'Snug in his own home.' (*Begins to cry.*)

Konstantin Nina—no— / stop.

Nina Take no notice, take no notice: it's good to cry. Yesterday evening I went to the back of the house to see if our theatre was still there. And there it was. So I cried. For the first time in two years I cried my heart out and it was good. Made things much much clearer. You see: I've stopped.

Takes his hand.

And look at *you*. A writer. You're a writer and I'm an actress. Not children any more. I don't wake up in my bed like I used to and start the day singing—no— tomorrow morning I'm getting up at half past five and catching the train with the peasants and their chickens to Yelyétz—and in Yelyétz there'll be the usual cultured clientele who assume 'actress' means—well, you can imagine.

Konstantin Why Yelyétz?

Nina Why not? I've signed up for the whole winter.

Pause.

I should go.

Konstantin When you left me, Nina, I suddenly felt so old—I turned into an old man—I hated being alive— I kept seeing your face—or I'd remember you under the tree—remember that night?—the elm?

Nina (*confused*) Why is he talking like this? Why is he / talking like this?

Konstantin Look at me: I've got nothing—nobody. I'm dead inside and everything I write is dead and cold and meaningless. Stay here—please—Nina—or let me come with you.
Why not, Nina? Why won't you?

Pause.

Nina I've got a cab waiting. Don't come. (*forcing herself not to cry*) Give me some water.

Konstantin (*gives her water*) Where is it you're going?

Nina Back to my hotel.

Pause.

What's your mother doing here?

Konstantin My uncle had an attack last Thursday. We sent a telegram.

Nina Why did you have to say that about the tree?

Arkádina and Trigorin laugh, off.

So it's him too. Oh well. Who cares. He said theatre was useless—kept making fun of me—kept chipping and chipping away till I felt useless myself—no confidence—second-rate—didn't know where to put my hands—couldn't act, couldn't stand right, couldn't control my voice. Horrible. I'm the seagull—is that right?—no. Remember? You shot one. 'Man turns up. Mindlessly destroys it. Idea for a story.' Is that right? No. (*Rubs her forehead.*) What was I saying? Oh yes: chipping away. But now I can really act—yes—really command the stage—feels amazing—like a drug. (*Slight pause.*) I've got to go. When I'm a real star, come and see me act. Promise? So . . . (*Squeezes his hand.*)

Konstantin Stay and have supper.

Nina No no—the cab—don't come. So she actually invited him to this house. Oh well. Who cares. I love him, Kostya. I love him more than ever. I want him. I can't bear it. I'm completely obsessed. Remember how innocent we were? Mmm? How good it felt? 'For millions of years.' Remember?

'For millions of years
now this earth is ash, this lake thick like mercury.
No boat lands on the empty shore.
No wading bird stands in the shallows.
And the moon—look—picks her way
like a looter through the ruined houses of the dead
slicing open her white fingers
on the sheets of smashed glass—
COLD
BLANK
DISTANT.'

She impulsively embraces Konstantin and goes out.

Slight pause.

Konstantin begins to tear up all his writing. After two silent minutes of this, he opens the locked door and goes out.

Dorn (*trying to open the door with the chair in front of it*) That's odd. Won't open. (*Pushes it open and replaces the chair.*) Huh. Musical chairs.

Enter Arkádina, Polina, then Yakov with bottles. Also Masha, Shamraev and Trigorin.

Arkádina The red wine and Aleksei's hot milk can go here on the table.

Polina (*to Yakov*) And bring us some coffee, would you?

They put on some music and begin to dance.

After a while, Shamraev and Yakov enter carrying a seagull in a glass cabinet. The dancing stops.

Shamraev This is the thing I was talking about. See? Your idea.

Trigorin (*looks at it*) I don't remember. (*Thinks.*) I don't remember.

A shot from the adjoining room. Everyone jumps.

Arkádina What was that?

Dorn Nothing. Sounds like the top's blown off a medicine bottle. Don't panic. (*Goes out and comes back half a minute later.*) I was right: it was my ether exploding. (*He starts humming, heading for some magazines, and Trigorin.*)

Arkádina (*sits at table*) My God. Terrifying. Just like when— (*Covers her face with her hands.*) Everything went black.

Dorn (*leafing through a magazine*) Did you read this thing they published a couple of months ago? . . . Very interesting discovery that was made . . . more in my domain than yours perhaps but . . .

With his arm around Trigorin he is leading him to the writing table.

Well . . . interesting all the same.
Get Irina out of here.

Trigorin What?

Dorn Just get her out. It's Konstantin—he's shot himself.

Note on This Version of *The Seagull*

This text was written for the National Theatre's 2006
production of the play, directed by Katie Mitchell, and
designed by Vicki Mortimer.

Written in 1895, the play looks back into the nineteenth
century and forward towards the twentieth. While this
is culturally fascinating, dramaturgically it is less so.
A choice was made therefore to strip away some of the
apparatus of nineteenth-century drama, with the aim
of making the play fully connect with a contemporary
audience. In practice this has meant reducing the
exposition, and cutting the asides and soliloquies.

To limit the 'exotic' effect of Russian names, each
character is given only a first name and a last name.
These names are used as in modern English.

In this imagining of the play, there are no true exterior
scenes. Act Two is set by Chekhov on a croquet lawn.
But in this version it takes place in the same (transformed)
dining room as Act Four. Restoring it to the croquet lawn
needs no change to the spoken text.

Act One is a little more complicated. The setting has
undergone a 180-degree rotation, so the actors don't
look upstage towards the lake, they look out towards the
auditorium. I include as an appendix the conventional
staging of Act One for anyone who wishes to reproduce
Chekhov's original scenic image.

MC, May 2006

Appendix

*The opening of Act One as originally
envisaged by Chekhov, with the lake upstage.*

*Evening. The garden of Sorin's estate. An avenue of
trees leads towards a lake. But a hastily constructed
stage conceals the lake from view.*

Medviedenko (*off*) And the way you dress—

Masha (*off*) What d'you mean: the way I dress?

Enter Masha and Medviedenko,

Medviedenko In black—why d'you always go round in
black?

Masha I'm in mourning for my life. I'm unhappy.

Medviedenko Oh? (*Slight pause.*) Then I'm confused.
You're healthy—your father's got money—not much
money but money all the same—while after deductions
I take home less than two hundred and fifty a month.
I lead a much harder life than you do, but I don't go
round in black.

Masha It's nothing to do with money. You can be poor
and still happy.

Medviedenko Well maybe in theory—but in practice it
goes like this: there's me, my mother, my two sisters and
my baby brother living on less than two hundred and
fifty a month. So what are you suggesting? Give up
smoking? Stop drinking tea? Or perhaps we could just /
not eat.

Masha The play should be starting soon.

Medviedenko Oh yes. Konstantin's play. Which Nina is going to act in. They're obsessed with each other and doing a play together is going to cement their relationship. Whereas the two of us don't even *have* a relationship. I love you, Masha, which is why I can't just sit at home vegetating. I walk here every day—two hours here, two hours back—and what's my reward?—total indifference. But of course, nobody wants to marry a man who can't provide.

Masha Rubbish. (*Lights cigarette.*) I'm touched by your love but I can't reciprocate, that's all. (*Offers cigarette.*) Want one?

Medviedenko Not in the mood.

Pause.

Masha It's close—feels like there'll be a storm tonight.
    It's just you're always picking away at things or talking about money. I know you think poverty's the biggest disaster in the world, but there are worse things in life than wandering the streets begging—believe me.
    I'm sorry. I know that's hard for you to understand.

Enter Sorin and Konstantin.

Konstantin I'm afraid we're not quite ready for you yet. I'm going to have to ask you both to leave. We'll call you when / it's time.

Sorin Masha—sweetheart—would you please please ask that father of yours to untie the dog so it doesn't howl. My sister spent the whole night awake again.

Masha Talk to my father yourself—it's not my job. And I'm not your sweetheart. (*to Medviedenko*) Come on— let's go.

Medviedenko (*to Konstantin*) You will tell us when it's going to start, yes?

Sorin Of course we will.

They go out.

So now that dog will be howling all night again.

Yakov Excuse me, sir—we're going for a swim.

Konstantin Alright—but I want you in position . . .
(*Looks at watch.*) . . . ten minutes from now.

Yakov You're the boss.

Yakov and workmen go out.

Konstantin So—what d'you think—empty space—no
scenery—just the lake and the horizon. Pure theatre. The
moon's due up at exactly half past eight—which is when
we start.

Sorin Excellent.

Konstantin And if Nina's late—which she looks like
being—then the whole effect's ruined. (*rearranging Sorin*)
Christ you're a mess. Can't you do something about this
hair?

Sorin It's the tragedy of my life. Even when I was young
I looked like an alcoholic. Complete failure with women.
  What's wrong with your mother?

Konstantin Wrong? She's bored. And she's jealous. She's
got it in for me and she's got it in for my play because
I've given the part to Nina and not to her. She hasn't
read my play of course but she already hates it.

Sorin (*laughs*) Come on: you're / overreacting.

Konstantin She can't bear the thought of Nina not her
getting all the attention—even in something so small
scale. Because it's not as if my mother isn't a sensitive
and intelligent person who genuinely cares about the
world—but try saying something nice to her about

71

another actress . . . big mistake. Nice things can be said *only about her*. Magazine features written *only about her*. She needs to have people constantly raving about her heartbreaking Cordelia or her 'waif-like' Juliet—and because out here in the country she's no way of feeding her addiction she gets bored and angry—we're all her enemies—we're all to blame. And talk about mean. We both know for a fact she's got a good seven hundred thousand stashed away in a Black Sea bank account—but ask her for money and she has a fit.

Sorin Come on—your mother worships you.

Konstantin (*laughs*) Worships me? I don't think so. She still sees herself as some kind of party-going *femme fatale*—but the problem is she's got a twenty-five-year-old son. When I'm not around she's only thirty-two—but when I'm here she's forty-three—and she hates me for it. Plus she knows I detest her darling theatre. She loves it—imagines it's her sacred contribution to society—but if you ask me this theatre of hers is death. When the curtain goes up on yet another adapted novel or some piece of vapid social commentary masquerading as art—when shouting and banging the scenery is mistaken for good acting—when writers think that dialogue means the fluent exchange of platitudes—when I see people churn out the same theatrical clichés time after time after time after time after time, then I want to scream and scream—like the man in Munch's picture.

Sorin We still need theatre.

Konstantin But we need to start again—if we can't start again from scratch—start again, make new forms—better to completely stop. (*Looks at watch.*) I love my mother—love her to death—but her life's meaningless—trailing round after her novelist-friend—name all over the papers—I'm sick of it. Yes, I realise some of it's egotistical: when I find myself thinking how much happier I'd be if she wasn't famous, if she was just a run-of-the-mill mother blah blah blah. And of course I used to feel so stupid when all her celebrity artist people turned up at her flat and I'd be the only nonentity —tolerated simply because I was her son. Because what could I say about myself? No special skills. No money. And because I'd been stupid enough to play politics at university, not even a degree. So when all these artists and writers deigned to show an interest I always knew that what they were actually doing was putting me in my place.

Sorin So what d'you make of this novelist friend? He doesn't say much.

Konstantin He's a nice enough person—hugely successful —but hardly a major talent. Put it this way—if you've read Tolstoy, you don't need to read Trigorin.

Sorin I'd be happy to settle for a minor talent—or any talent at all come to / think of it.

Konstantin Listen! (*Hugs his uncle.*) She's incredible. Even her footsteps sound beautiful—don't you think?

 Nina enters.

Nina . . . You look amazing.

Nina Am I late? Promise me I'm not late—

Konstantin No no no no no . . .

Nina I've been worrying all day—I was so scared. I thought my father would stop me coming—then he and my stepmother went out. The sky's red—the moon's already rising—and there's me driving the horse on and on and on . . . (*Laughs.*) I'm so happy. (*Squeezes Sorin's hand.*)

Sorin Those pretty eyes look more like they've been crying.

Nina It's nothing—just out of breath—in half an hour I need to get back—so please let's hurry—please—please don't make me late—my father doesn't know I'm here.

Konstantin Then let's call everyone and start.

Sorin Let me. (*He moves off, humming.*)

Nina I shouldn't be here. They think I'll be corrupted. But I'm drawn here to the lake—like a seagull. (*Looks around.*)

Konstantin We're alone.

Nina Somebody's there.

Konstantin No one.

They kiss.

Nina What's that tree?

Konstantin An elm.

Nina Why's it so dark?

Konstantin It's evening—everything's dark. Please stay for longer.

Nina No.

Konstantin Or I could come to your house.

Nina No.

Konstantin I love you.

Nina Shh . . .

Someone is heard behind the stage.

Konstantin Yakov?

Yakov (*off*) Yes sir?

Konstantin Final checks, please. We're about to start.

Yakov (*off*) Yes sir.

Konstantin And remember: the sulphur and the red eyes have the same cue. (*to Nina*) Nervous?

Nina Very. It's not so much your mother—but acting in front of Aleksei Trigorin—the writer—I'm terrified. He's so famous. Is he young?

Konstantin Yes.

Nina His stories are wonderful.

Konstantin (*cold*) Are they? I've never read them.

Nina Your play's so difficult to act. My character's not real.

Konstantin Not real? I've told you: the material world is an illusion—what counts is the world of dreams.

Nina And nothing really happens—it's all talking.

They move off.

And I'm not sure a play's really a play unless it has some kind of message . . . Don't you think? . . .

They both go off behind the stage.

Konstantin (*off*) A message?

Nina (*off*) Yes. About love or . . . I don't know . . . people's feelings . . . relationships.

Konstantin laughs.

Why's that funny? . . .

Enter Polina and Dorn.

Polina It's getting damp. Go back and get your overcoat.

Dorn I'm hot.

Polina Why won't you look after yourself? You're so stubborn. You know damp air's bad for you, but you just like making me worry. Yesterday you spent the whole evening out on that terrace quite deliberately . . .

Dorn hums a little tune.

. . . but I suppose you found your little conversation with Irina Arkádina so totally fascinating you didn't notice the cold. Am I right?

Dorn I'm fifty-five.

Polina So? That's not old for a man. You certainly don't look old and women still find you attractive—as you very well know.

Dorn So what are you suggesting I do?

Polina Why're men all so obsessed by actresses? Mmm?

Dorn (*hums a little tune, then*) If people idealise performers and tend to treat them differently from— say—pig-farmers, then that's just how the world operates. It's outside of our control.

Polina Women have always been all over you—I suppose you can't control that either.

Dorn (*shrugs*) What if they have? Women 've always been very good to me—of course—but mainly because they could trust me professionally. Ten, fifteen years ago, as you very well know, I was the only reliable obstetrician this district had. It doesn't mean I've abandoned you. Or Masha either.

Polina (*grasps his hand*) I'm sorry. I know you haven't.

Dorn Don't. Someone's coming. (*He frees his hand.*)

Enter Arkádina, Sorin, Trigorin, Shamraev, Medviedenko and Masha.

Shamraev You should've seen her when was it—fifteen— no I tell a lie—twenty—it was twenty years ago I first saw you at the Poltava Agricultural Show. Amazing acting. Even in a place like that. And that colleague of yours—the comic actor—Pavel something—brilliant in Ostrovsky—Pavel Chadin—whatever happened to him?

Arkádina You keep asking me about dinosaurs. How should I know?

Shamraev Chadin . . . Pavel Chadin. There's no one like that left. The theatre's gone downhill. In the past there were mighty oaks—now all we see are the stumps.

Dorn There may be fewer geniuses about, but the average actor has significantly improved.

Shamraev I don't agree. Still—it's a matter of taste. For which—as the poet says—there is no accounting.

Konstantin comes out from behind the stage.

Arkádina Aren't you starting?

Konstantin One more minute. Give me a chance.

Arkádina
   'What have I done, that thou dar'st wag thy tongue
   In noise so rude against me?'

Konstantin
               'Such an act
   That blurs the grace and blush of modesty.'

Yakov makes a sound cue.

Ready everyone? Then let's begin.

   Spirits
   night-time spirits of the lake
   rock us asleep and let us dream
   of things a hundred million years from now.

Sorin A hundred million years from now there won't be anything.

Konstantin Then let's see what not anything looks like.

Arkádina Yes let's. We're asleep.

The curtain opens, revealing Nina—and, beyond her, the lake and the rising moon.

Nina

Everything human, everything animal, every plant,
stem, green tendril, blade of grass—
each living cell
has divided and divided and divided
and died.
For millions of years
now this earth is ash, this lake thick like mercury.
No boat lands on the empty shore.
No wading bird stands in the shallows.
And the moon—look—picks her way
like a looter through the ruined houses of the dead
slicing open her white fingers
on the sheets of smashed glass—
COLD
BLANK
DISTANT.

Pause.

The brutal material struggle of individuals has ended.
Only the steady heartbeat of the world goes on.
I am that heartbeat.
I am the blood moving under the skin.
I am the slow pulse of the universal will.

Marsh lights appear.

Arkádina (*sotto voce*) Is this one of those experimental
things?

Konstantin Mother!

Nina

I am alone.
Once in a hundred thousand years I try to speak
but my mouth fills with brick-dust and broken glass.
Nobody hears me:
not the moon
not the pale fires ringing the cracked horizon—

billions of atoms chaotically changing.
Only the steady heart-beat of the world does not change.
SLOW
DEEP
IMPLACABLE.

Pause.
A cloud of gas is released.
Two red spots appear against the background of the lake.

And now my enemy approaches:
the violent Other—
origin of material brutality.

I can hear his body
   churn the lake—
smell his foul breath.
I can see his terrifying
   lidless eyes.
The violent Other:
hoping to wind the
   steel wire of reason
round my white throat.

Arkádina I can smell sulphur. Is that intentional?

Konstantin Yes.

Arkádina (*laughs*) Of course—it's a special effect!

Konstantin Mother!

Polina (*to Dorn*) Why did you take your hat off? Put it back on or you'll catch cold.

HARD
BITTER
RESTLESS.

Arkádina The doctor is doffing his hat to the violent Other, origin of / material brutality.

Konstantin Stop! Stop the play!

Arkádina What're you so / angry about?

Konstantin Stop the play! Stop it now! Stop!

The curtain is closed.

Forgive me. I forgot that writing and acting is the privilege of the chosen few—whose monopoly I've somehow infringed. But I . . . I . . . (*He struggles to speak, makes a gesture—'Why bother?'—and goes out.*)

Arkádina What on earth is he talking about?

Sorin Sweetheart—you hurt his pride.

. . . and continuing from the foot of page 14 above to end of scene.